The background and creation of the
IPSWICH CHARTER HANGINGS

The background and creation of the
IPSWICH CHARTER HANGINGS

by Isabel Clover

Foreword by Dr John Blatchly

Introduced by Professor Chris Green OBE
Chairman of Ipswich Arts Association

Ipswich Arts Association
2003

First published 2003
Produced and published by
Ipswich Arts Association
The Town Hall
Ipswich, Suffolk. IP1 1BZ
www.ipswich-arts.org.uk

Map © Ferial Rogers 2003
Photographs of the
Charter Hangings by Keith Locke
Designed by Jonathan Green
Printed by Gipping Press Ltd
ISBN 0-9546324-0-0

Foreword
Dr John Blatchly

Anything which reminds the Ipswich people and visitors to our town of its proud past does a great service, for not all of us can discern for ourselves unaided the legacy of past centuries. We need encouragement to develop the seeing eye and questioning mind. Many fine things remain to be enjoyed, and from pictures and prints we know plenty about buildings and artefacts no longer surviving. Those who have already seen the Charter Hangings realise that Isabel Clover and her teams of embroiderers have made for our delight and instruction eight of the richest and most revealing embroideries as any in the country. Each of these jewel-like works of art covers about a century, capacious pigeon-holes for our knowledge of that period. A simple map shows two things about the town. The early tenth-century ramparts, roughly circular, surrounding the much older lattice of roads, survive to a remarkable extent. Ipswich sits on its river, Gipping becoming Orwell at Stoke Bridge, like a ball poised on the edge of a weir.

Even before this book was produced every inhabitant of the town could have invested in the set of eight postcards of the hangings as their own aide-memoire, for new secrets of the panels are revealed at each fresh viewing. Put them in a simple frame about 17 cm by 90 cm and the slowly-flowing river which unites the whole can then be appreciated; how various is its marine life. The hangings work on three distinct levels: as fine works of art of masterly composition, as a pageant of the town's history and as a display of embroidering techniques. The presiding genius, Isabel herself, writes about the last two in later chapters.

Architectural styles are splendidly and economically represented, and just as some of the earlier buildings are now lost, some in the latest panel are destined to follow the same fate. Agriculture has a place in most but not all periods. The eighth hanging reflects the comparatively secular nature of our present age but in the earlier ones religious references abound, with the denominations treated even-handedly. Heraldry and other artefacts rich in symbolism such as seals, coins and merchants' marks, are generously represented among the many images in these Charter Hangings. A few worthies are represented amongst the tiny figures; others live through their coats of arms and trade-marks. A keen eye, and the explanation section, will reward the curious so that no image need remain an enigma.

It hardly matters that St Matthew's West Gate and North Gate are shown in later hangings: they were, of course, medieval. How splendid that our theatre will always be the plain Wolsey Theatre in the last panel, and that there was room for Norman Foster's pioneering Willis building, plenty of transport history and the great sweep of the Orwell Bridge.

Why the Charter Hangings?
Professor Christopher Green

Welcome to the Ipswich Charter Hangings! I hope this book will add to your enjoyment and appreciation of these wonderful works of art. As Chairman of the Ipswich Arts Association I would like to tell you a little of the background to this magnificent achievement. At a discussion within Ipswich Arts about a suitable way to celebrate 800 years since the granting of a Royal Charter to Ipswich by King John in 1200, my colleague, Ferial Rogers, suggested a tapestry of some kind. Tapestries or other embroidered hangings have long been a means of commemorating important events, the Bayeux Tapestry being a famous example. We thought it would be a simple matter of a few sketches, some nimble hands and a few months in the creation. That was a fantasy of epic proportions!

We turned to Isabel Clover, a lecturer and tutor at Suffolk College and known nationally for her ecclesiastical designs and embroidery. She set about the historical research and suggested eight embroidered hangings, one for each century since the Charter, which seemed logical, although later that plan was revised to include the period in Ipswich pre-dating the Charter. Isabel calculated that the cost of materials for each panel would be about £500 and so I set about getting sponsorship and was delighted with the response.

Isabel gathered around her a team of past and present City and Guild students who would produce the various parts of each hanging, and started work on detailed designs. As the 800th Charter anniversary approached the first hanging was shown at the John Russell Gallery to admiration and critical acclaim. With each subsequent panel the intricate work seemed to be ever more breathtaking, the detail, colour and general glory ever more apparent. Isabel had to bear the brunt of a long and very taxing schedule, along with her teams. Literally hundreds of hours have gone into the production of each hanging and it took just over three years to research, design and complete all eight.

They have been seen by thousands of people at the individual exhibitions at the John Russell Gallery, at the opening complete display at the Graham & Oldham Artist's Gallery, and subsequently at Ipswich Museum and the Cathedral at Bury St Edmunds. We are currently planning an exhibition in Arras, our French partner town. We now urgently need to find a permanent home for the Charter Hangings in Ipswich. When mounted and glazed they need a large space to be seen to their full advantage. They are designed to be viewed in a continuous line, with the River Orwell running through them. They must be kept in a public space because it is the intention of the Ipswich Arts Association to give them to the people of Ipswich.

In the meantime I shall endeavour to keep these superb works of art on public display as often as possible. They are a magnificent commemoration of 800 years of Ipswich history, and will be part of our heritage for the future. To Isabel and her teams; to my colleagues in the Ipswich Arts Association; to all the volunteers, well-wishers and sponsors who have helped the idea come to fruition; and to you, for supporting the Charter Hangings and reading this book, I am most profoundly grateful.

The Medieval Town. Detail evoking the density of the historic centre.

Researching and Designing the Charter Hangings
Isabel Clover

I was commissioned by Ipswich Arts Association to undertake the task of researching, designing and directing the Charter Hangings. It would have been a more difficult task if I had not been born and brought up in Ipswich with a passion for history. Originally the idea was for six panels, which swiftly grew to eight. I started with a set of very small-scale sketches in black and white which were presented to the IAA and accepted in principle. The task of turning the small sketches into full drawings began and the real work started.

I envisaged them as a continuous whole, with the River Orwell flowing through and each panel framed with an arch appropriate to the period of history enclosed within it. I wanted to use buildings wherever possible that still existed and to celebrate some interesting buildings that no longer remain, such as St Mildred's Church. The idea was to give an overall feel for the different periods and illustrate as many of the different activities and historical facts as possible. I hoped to excite the people of Ipswich with the rich history of our town and to provide tourists with a new way to appreciate it too.

A great deal of research went into each panel and I am so grateful for all the help I received. At the Mayor's Parlour I was able to handle and draw the Corporation seal (now called the Borough seal) which appears in the Medieval panel, and find the thirteenth century interpretation of St Mildred's Church on the first hanging, or panel, on its reverse side. Keith Wade, the County Archaeologist helped me with the first panel, producing early Viking illustrations. Dr Steven Plunkett of Ipswich Museum Service talked to me about the pre-Charter period and suggested I keep the focus of the hanging to around the time of the Norman Invasion. The last Viking raid on Ipswich was 1069, hence the Viking boat depicted in the centre of the first panel.

Research for the subsequent panels took me to the Suffolk Record Office, Christchurch Mansion and Ipswich Museum, where I am particularly grateful to David Jones, Keeper of Mankind at the Museum for his enthusiasm, time and patience. The description beside each panel gives details of where the many different artefacts come from although, as wider inspiration for the Charter and Medieval panels, I sought out relevant manuscripts of the period to add contemporary atmosphere. For example, the large merchant's boat on the left in the second hanging is the boat bringing Thomas à Becket back from exile in France taken from an early thirteenth century illuminated manuscript of the life of Thomas à Becket. In a mid- fourteenth century version of the Ipswich Little Domesday I was delighted to discover the three grotesque faces which appear in the third hanging, probably illustrations by the clerk of locals.

Charter Hanging: pencil drawing & detail of Corporation seal. The drawing was made of the seal, and is therefore a mirror image of the imprint.

John Knapp and his wife in the Stuart Hanging came from a brass in St Peter's Church. A painting by Samuel Read in Ipswich Museums collection was the source for buildings in the Georgian Hanging, particularly the weighbridge and the medieval Custom House. A photograph in the Burrows collection at the Record Office was the source for the provision market. The plough and the lawnmower in the Victorian hanging are from an old Ransome's catalogue in Ipswich Museum, the slums from a painting by Frederick Brett Russel in the Ipswich Museums collection. All existing buildings are based on photographs taken by myself and one of the team walking around the town. These are just a few examples of where my research led me.

In designing the hangings I tried to create the atmosphere of each period. The buildings were chosen symbolically and not placed in their actual position in the town but in order to create a pattern of the period, reflecting the two centres of the town: the Cornhill and the docks. In the Medieval Hanging, for example, the buildings are placed to give a crowded feel to the town, and, although the St Lawrence church tower is not right for the period, I have used artistic licence as it is so decorative.

A team was recruited and as the design for the first panel was completed discussions took place with the team on actually starting the work. Colours were discussed and fabrics chosen. The problem of natural dyes fading made it important to use commercially dyed fabrics as much as possible. The river was one of our first discussion points and here we decided to use silk velvet dyed with silk dyes. We realised that the colour might change in time but this would be acceptable as the river flowing through all the panels changes from dark to light, according to the level of pollution.

The team was not made up of volunteers but of people who were chosen because they were able to work closely together. I had the final word as the hangings needed a professional overview to maintain a unity. Different teams and different people joining the work stretched the standard of excellence further, but there had to be a strong lead to achieve an overall professional standard.

The best way to describe how the process worked is to imagine making a giant jigsaw puzzle. Each piece was given to the person whose style of work was most suited to that item. We had meetings of as many of the team as possible at regular intervals to compare the work and progress it further. Particular skill is needed for gold work, which was carried out by my church embroidery students who have many years' experience between them. When the different pieces were completed they had to be sewn in and this brought in a new team who assembled the panels. More detail was then added. As we moved on to the third panel, work became more and more complicated. Each person had a design to follow but keeping the work exactly the right size was sometimes difficult, especially when the jigsaw was assembled.

When I saw the completed hangings I was relieved, exhausted and deeply grateful for the immense work and loyalty to the project of the team, and amazed that we had all survived!

The Embroidery

The hangings are embroidered by hand and machine stitchery with *appliqué*, quilting and gold work, raised and padded in relief in rich colours and embellished with gold. We tried to use techniques that were right for each period whenever possible, until the twentieth century. At this time techniques changed with the advent of the sewing machine in the 1840s and modern new materials became available.

In the beginning I made large-scale drawings, then tracings were carefully made of each piece and given to the person most suited to the style of work needed. The techniques were discussed, fabrics and threads chosen and colours agreed – these were monitored very frequently at group meetings. Each hanging produced a range of technical problems. It was always important that the colours should flow across the whole set and that similar techniques should be used across all the panels.

The use of gold thread was important for the heraldic and ecclesiastical work and this needed to be continued across the panels until the twentieth –century one. Here we used modern holographic, bonded plastic fabric to simulate glass buildings and give light to the work. As we worked further into the project the panels became more complicated and sewing in became a bit of a nightmare – not because things did not fit, this was rarely a problem, but the right pieces were not always ready in order to assemble them. Each panel was assembled in Suffolk College.

Linen was chosen as the background for the first hanging and the pattern of the coins stamped on to it in silver acrylic paint. The coins themselves are embroidered on top of applied shot grey taffeta in chain stitch with larger areas in silver padded kid. The little deer is padded leather on to blue linen which also needed to be padded and is surrounded by a machine-made braid which is also the cord for the Viking knot. The clasp shown at the end of the knot is of coral seed beads from a dismantled necklace, embellished with a broken watch-strap. St Mildred's Church is in traditional gold work with laid gold, bead purl and padded leather. The Viking ship is handmade felt covered in black net, cut through and quilted on the machine. The shields are paper and tissue embossed with foil onto leather; the rudder is the inside of a tomato puree tube, beaten flat and cut into shape.

Making a wild boar is quite a problem, but a new pliable copper wire mesh is now available and very useful for 3D work and *papier mâché*. The moulded boar was covered in layers of tissue paper and machine-embroidered, dyed muslin then put on top of that and stitched in.

The Charter panel itself needed to have the feel of a medieval manuscript, and rich, long- piled blue velvet was chosen. Small, embroidered squares of cotton gauze were added, to give the impression of a medieval carpet page. The ships, glistening in layers of metallic organza were quilted on the machine and slashed to reveal the colours underneath. The top corner has an illumination from the Charter of Edward III in the Record Office and the embroidery was done in the traditional Opus Anglicanum technique of split stitch, laid gold threads and padded kid. Another traditional technique, basket work, was used on the Corporation seal, which was estimated to have taken over 200 hours to complete. Velvet, bonded in chiffon over layers of paint, was machine-embroidered to make stonework, and the arches in the middle cut through to reveal other fabrics underneath.

The Medieval Hanging was the beginning of difficult challenges. There were many more buildings to depict in a period of growth and prosperity for the town. The need for very accurate sewing started at this point, as even 1/8 inch too small or large throws out the whole plan. A problem also arose because everyone does not work at the same speed or have the same amount of spare time. We behaved as professionals although the team was a group of selected volunteers. Stitching in the pieces for the Medieval Hanging was very complicated and took much longer than was anticipated. From then on the assembly took longer and longer as the detail got more intricate.

The church was made by three different people. The stonework is in *papier mâché* with stones painted in. The windows are bonded fabrics in chiffon and the decorative flintwork in felt . The Staple seal, on the right, shows the Pascal Lamb worked in bullion knots on to a sail of red felt, standing on a ship worked in *or nué*. The gateway to Archdeacon Pykenham's house is painstakingly darned with stranded cotton on scrim but canvas work has been used on others of this type with pleated organza for roofs. The fields at the bottom are felt, layered with nylon organza, machined and slashed, although some are painted canvas with scattered stitching and the sheep are in manipulated gloving leather.

The Tudor hanging was really taxing again because of the wealth of buildings to record and the large number of artefacts in the Museum to draw on. The timber- framed buildings introduced in the third panel were very important in the Tudor period, very thick handmade paper gessoed on to the muslin is used with leather for the beams, roofs become layers of threads machined together. The background for this hanging is not in one piece, but different layers applied to the centre ground. Small pieces of velvet and silk make up the *appliqué* for the little figures in the procession, while the clergy carry a cross of twisted wire wrapped with gold threads.

The River Orwell is a unifying factor as it flows through all eight hangings. From now on all the ships were to be leather as it gave firm, sharp lines. They were pieced together on to pelmet vilene with washers, cords, wrapped cocktail sticks and even barbecue skewers added for the masts. I had a real problem when I thought that the hanging was becoming too red, but it all balanced out in the end.

The first hanging was based on a strong plain background of strong colour, and it was necessary to repeat this in the fifth, the Stuarts, which also gives the eye a rest from so much detail. The top part of this panel is deliberately plain to reflect the Puritan period. The buildings now had a technique to follow but at the bottom of this panel we had to create the Ancient House (Sparrowe's House). Tea-dyed muslin knotted tightly was used for the swags. Tiny cavaliers talk in the cheese and butter markets, all put together with machine *appliqué* on a variety of fabrics, such as velvet, silk, feathers, cords and leather. The fish stall on the left has tiny fish hanging on the stall, with a Puritan cleric in work clothing chatting to a lady who is shopping. The rich merchant and his wife, on the edge of the panel, are dressed in damask and fur. The new coat of arms awarded to the town at the Restoration was a challenge. The seahorse supporters to the arms are in silver pelmet vilene with silver lurex mesh. The metallic gauze fins are smocked on a pleating machine.

Gold work is used in the top corners of the Georgian panel, this time for the inside of a clock. Clocks were very important to the town economy at the time. The Moore clock on the left is meticulously painted with acrylic paint on leather. The Unitarian church at the top has the most beautiful pulpit, carefully recorded in manipulated organza. The lower part of the panel has handmade felt from my Shetland sheep. There is a very large painting in Ipswich Town Hall which inspired the garden/allotment on the other side of the river and the plants are stitched in different wools.

Buildings are difficult to portray in embroidery. The nature of textiles is soft and malleable, obviously the opposite is true of buildings. Colour became a problem as we reached the Victorian hanging, for as Tudor brickwork disappeared, buildings tended to become more grey. The new Custom house in the seventh hanging helped to add colour. Previously the side of the docks had been done in canvas work with very small pieces of snakeskin, but by this time the area had been tidied up and so we used a different colour and stitch. Giving similar pieces of work throughout the panels to the same people helped with continuity of style.

At the top of the Victorian panel the new Town Hall was difficult to reproduce but layers of commercial felt and painted vilene with stitches in stranded cotton provided the solution. The arch over the whole panel is grey velvet giving the appearance of stone. A piece of faded velvet used for the brickwork of the new tower for Ipswich School gives an interesting texture. The Victorians loved velvet and we found it so useful for many things on this panel, including County Hall. The barges are heavy painted leather with dyed muslin folded for the furled sails.

The last hanging has so much glass the multi-coloured holograph, bonded plastic fabric was excellent in giving a good impression of it. We buried it under different shades of coloured chiffon to look like reflected light which kept the play of light we had achieved with gold and silver threads in the earlier hangings.

Where did we get the fabrics? Well, everywhere. On the whole we bought enough for all the hangings but it would have been impossible to find some of the tiny pieces which one assembles over a lifetime and these were kindly donated by the team.

We all hope the Charter Hangings will continue to be enjoyed for many years to come.

Tudor period: Spandrel carvings of, this page, St. Michael the archangel, and opposite, the Dragon.

Map by Ferial Rogers

Siting historical buildings featured in the hangings

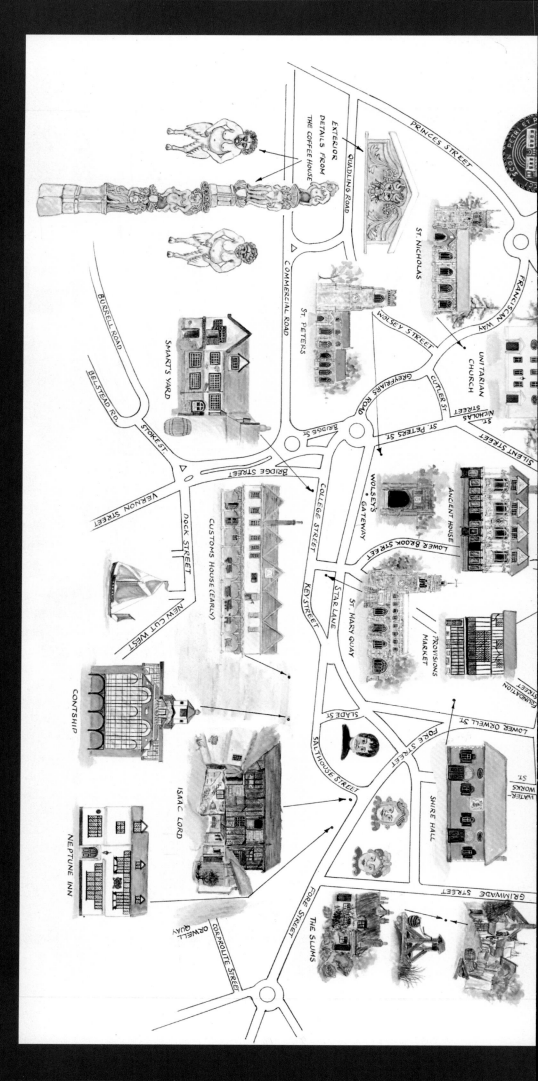

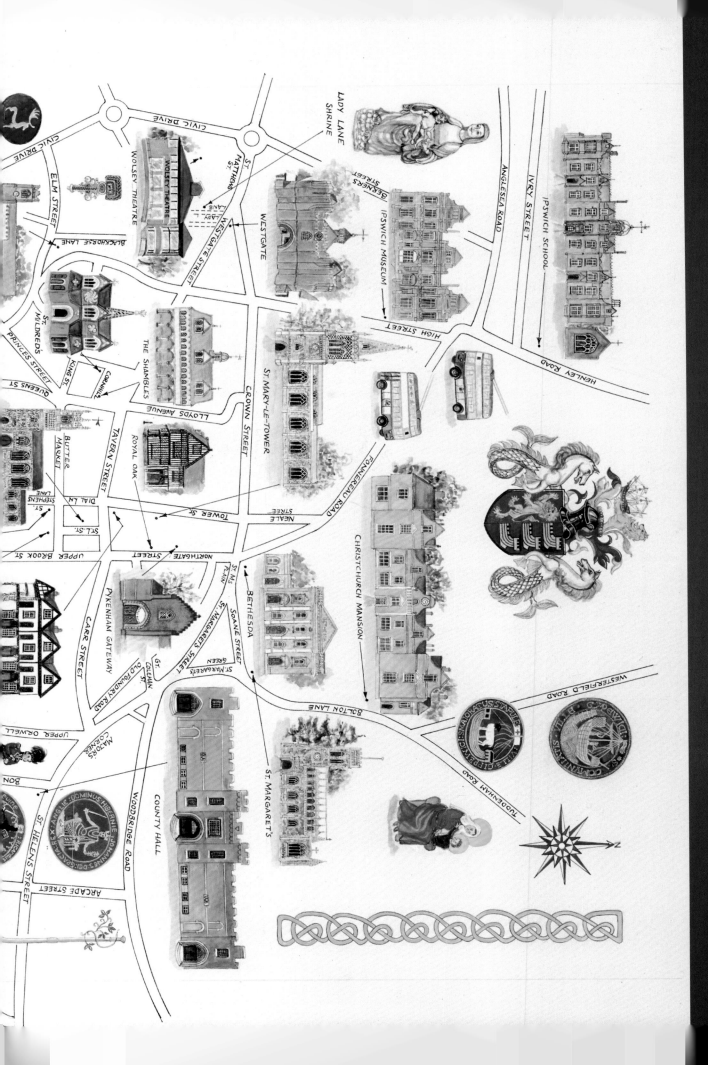

CIVIC DRIVE

CIVIC DRIVE

ELM STREET

BLACKHORSE LANE

WOLSEY THEATRE

WOLSEY THEATRE

ST. MATTHEWS ST.

CIVIC DRIVE

LADY LANE

WESTGATE STREET

WESTGATE

LADY LANE SHRINE

BERNERS STREET

ST. MILDREDS

PRINCES STREET

KING ST.

CORNHILL

THE SHAMBLES

LLOYDS AVENUE

QUEENS ST

ROYAL OAK

CROWN STREET

ST. MARY-LE-TOWER

IPSWICH MUSEUM

HIGH STREET

ANGLESEA ROAD

IVRY STREET

IPSWICH SCHOOL

HENLEY ROAD

BUTTER MARKET

TAVERN STREET

DIAL LN.

ST. STEPHENS LANE

ST. ST.

UPPER BROOK ST.

NORTHGATE STREET

TOWER ST.

NEALE STREET

FONNEREAU ROAD

CHRISTCHURCH MANSION

PYKENHAM GATEWAY

CARR STREET

OLD FOUNDRY ROAD

ST. M.S. PL.AN.

ST. MARGARET'S STREET

COLEMAN ST.

GT. COLEMAN ST.

SOANE STREET

BETHESDA

ST.MARGARETS GREEN

GT. ST.MARGARETS GREEN

BOLTON LANE

WESTERFIELD ROAD

UPPER ORWELL

MAJORS CORNER

ST. MARGARET'S

TUDDENHAM ROAD

DON

ST. HELENS STREET

WOODBRIDGE ROAD

COUNTY HALL

ARCADE STREET

N

Ipswich before its first Royal Charter

This hanging assembles images of the town's importance in Anglo-Saxon times.

The town of Gipeswic (Ipswich) owes its foundation to the house of Raedwald, who was buried at Sutton Hoo and had his royal dwelling near Woodbridge. The bronze deer in the top left corner crowns the whetstone sceptre found among his grave goods. The sixth century Anglo-Saxon brooch (lower left), excavated at the Hadleigh Road cemetery, is now in Ipswich Museum. The centre of the town was newly laid out by Raedwald's kinsman King AElfwald during the eighth century.

Ipswich was sacked by the Vikings on several occasions, perhaps as early as 841 and certainly as late as 1069. The Viking boat is drawn from a gravestone in Stora Hammers, Sweden, as is the figure with the torch, here adapted to represent a protector and defender of Gipeswic. The knot pattern on the left comes from the same gravestone.

The church is from the Corporation seal of 1200 and may depict the church of St Mildred, which stood from the eighth century on the site of the present Town Hall on the Cornhill. Coins were minted in Gipeswic from the eighth century, and Ipswich-struck coins have been found all over Europe. Those shown to the left of the church, of King Ethelred the Unready, can be seen in Ipswich Museum.

Below the river the boar (left) is taken from the early twelfth -century stone tympanum from a doorway into the lost church of All Saints; it is now in St Nicholas' church. Beside it, St Michael fights the dragon of the Apocalypse, also now in St Nicholas' church. The monastic seal (top right) is that of the Augustinian priory of St Peter and St Paul which covered six acres north and east of St Peter's church. The arch surrounding the panel evokes the south door to St Mary Elms church, perhaps preserved from the now lost church of St Saviour.

The River Orwell flows through each of the panels to emphasise its importance to the continuity of the town's history.

The Charter Hanging

The Royal Charter which King John sent to Ipswich from Normandy in June 1200 was the first to give the townspeople control over their own affairs. Two bailiffs, twelve portmen and twenty-four common councilmen were elected on 8 September every year to form the Corporation; it was only in 1835 that these offices were changed to mayor, aldermen and councillors.

At the top of the panel under the Norman round-headed arch are three seals. The Corporation seal at the top is taken from an original impression made in 1200 and now kept in the Mayor's Parlour. Below are the seals of King John on the left and his elder brother King Richard on the right. The original Charter of King John was stolen by the town clerk but subsequent charters exist, including one of Edward III (now in the Suffolk Record Office), the illumination from which is celebrated at the top of the hanging. The background pattern of lozenges is found in medieval manuscripts.

On the right-hand side is the moot horn which was used to call the Corporation to meetings. Although it is purported to have been given to the borough by King John in 1200, it is of Anglo-Saxon origin and now in Ipswich Museum.

The importance and wealth of Ipswich came from trade through its port. The Ipswich 'cat' (with the first ever movable rudder) can be seen in the centre on the river. On the right a merchant is being rowed to his large ship on the left. He holds a coin in his hand ready to pay his fare.

At the bottom are Norman cloisters of the kind that may have been found in the Augustinian priory of St Peter and St Paul, founded about 1130 near Stoke Bridge. The apostle is just one of several on a stone screen in St Nicholas' Church.

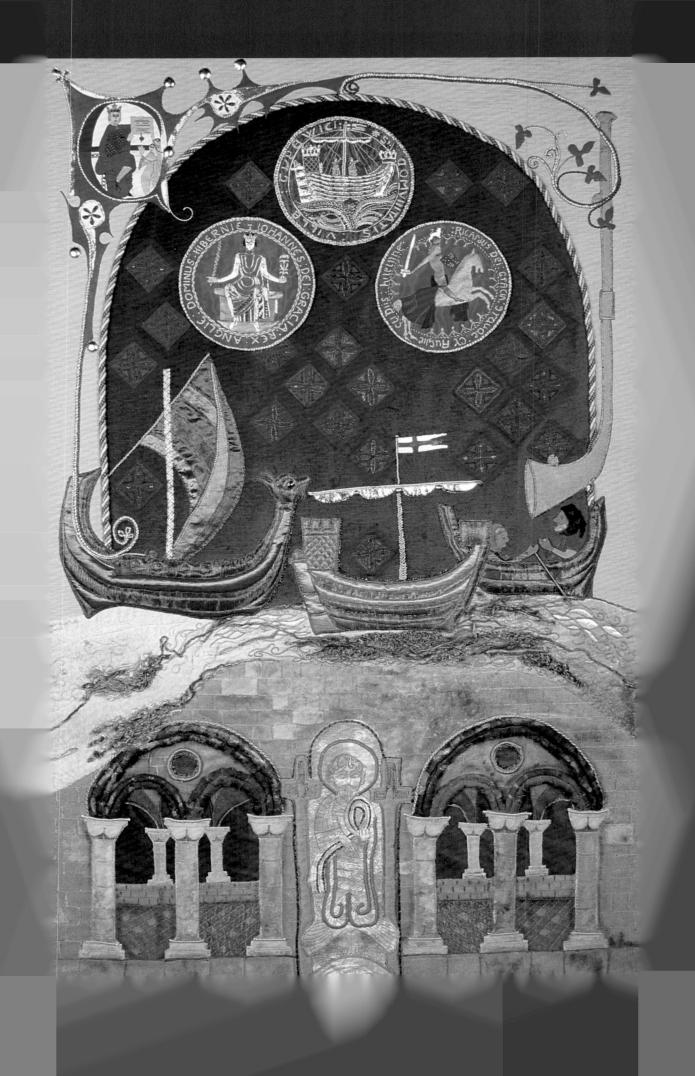

The Medieval Town

Ipswich must have been glorious at this time. There were more than a dozen medieval churches and many amazing buildings which unfortunately have been destroyed in the modernisation of the town.

The arches represent the Early English style. Within the left-hand arch is a cross section of the roof of St Margaret's Church, the finest double hammerbeam roof in Ipswich. The decorative corner above to the left has the merchant's mark of John Hall, dyer, who paid for the roof and clerestory of St Margaret's . The shield in the centre is the badge of the Augustinian Priory of Holy Trinity or Christchurch which stood outside the North Gate where Christchurch Mansion is today. In the top right corner are the clothier's shears from the roof of the Clothe Hall which stood in Star Lane near the Quay.

Beside the river are some of the town buildings of the period. At the front are depicted the cottages behind St Mary Elms. To the left is the Isaac Lord warehouse. Behind them is the Moot Hall which stood on the Cornhill on the site of the present Town Hall. This court for the town, built in the late fourteenth century, incorporated parts of St Mildred's Church, seen on the first hanging. Behind the hall on the right is Pykenham's Gateway which led to the mansion of the Archdeacon (opposite the Central Library near the North Gate). In the background is the tower of St Lawrence Church with its decorative flint flushwork: it is in fact Victorian designed to a medieval ideal.

Under the right-hand arch is the statue of Our Lady of Grace from the famous chapel shrine which stood in Lady Lane and was as great a pilgrimage site as Walsingham. A modern bronze statue now celebrates the site. The Staple seal beneath (now in the Museum) was used from 1364 to guarantee the quality of cloth for export. The Staple warehouse held goods until the tolls had been claimed.

Below the seal the Church of St Mary at the Quay was chosen as the waterside church where the Ipswich merchants Thomas Pownder (1525) and Henry 'Great' Tooley (1551) were buried.

On the right-hand edge of the panel, beside the seal of the Staple, is the corner post from the Fox and Goose tavern which was in Foundation Street. On the opposite side are details of a post from the corner of Cox Lane.

On the river is a warship built here for Edward I, also a small fishing coracle. The small boat to the right represents the importance of the river trade at the time, particularly in wine (the boatman is drinking out of a large goblet!). The fish below come from a medieval manuscript.

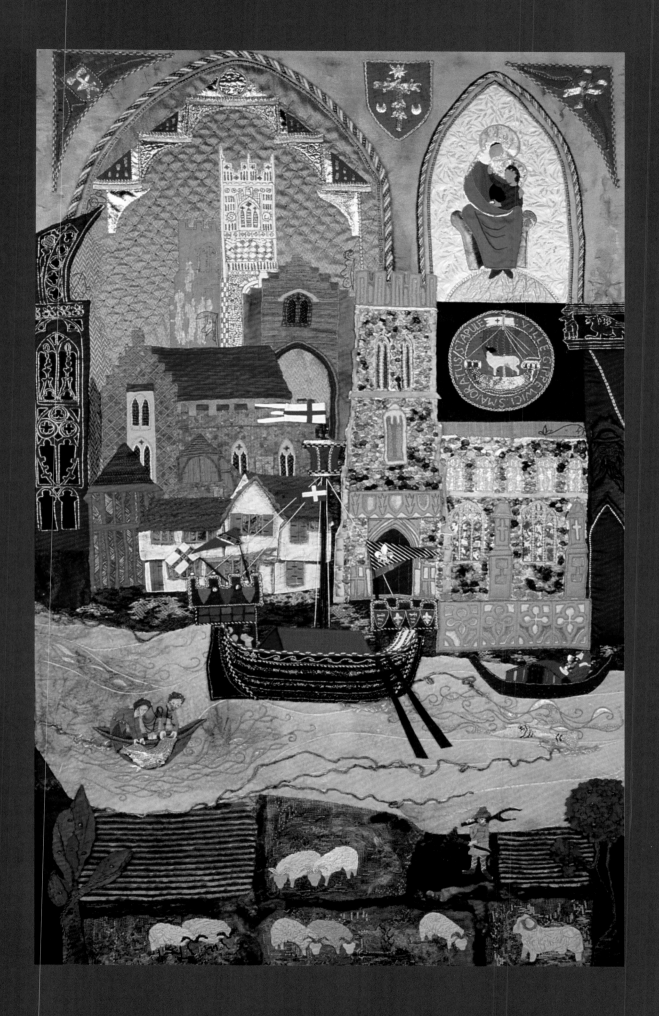

The Tudor Period

At the beginning of the Tudor period Ipswich was still Catholic. Many pilgrims came to the town to visit the shrine of Our Lady of Ipswich, even the royal pilgrims Henry VIII and Katherine of Aragon. At the top of the hanging, clergy and townspeople process to the shrine. Ipswich was the birthplace of Cardinal Thomas Wolsey, and his coat of arms is at the top, surmounted by his cardinal's hat; while at the bottom of the post, on the left, a butcher's boy with a knife in his mouth reminds us that Wolsey's father was a butcher. Next to him is all that remains of his grand plan for a college: a waterside gateway.

At the top of the panel are two spandrel carvings, St Michael the archangel on the right and the Dragon on the left. They were carved on the entrance to the White Hart which stood on the site of Brook Street Craft Market.

On the Cornhill stood the Market Cross, removed in 1812. Two carved and painted heads top the corner posts on each side of the hanging. The post on the left comes from Brown's Yard, that on the right from an inn opposite the Ancient House in Dial Lane. Both are now in the Museum.

The Shambles (slaughter house) stood on Cornhill and below this is the Royal Oak, still standing in Northgate Street at the corner of Oak Lane. During this time of religious strife martyrs were burned on the Cornhill; groups are shown suffering on either side of the market cross.

Large new properties were erected on sites of religious houses suppressed or dissolved by Henry VIII. Christchurch, built on the site of the Augustinian Priory, is shown at the top of the hanging, with two of its original knot gardens in front. The mansion is now part of Ipswich Museum. Below it is the tower of the Great Place built for Sir Thomas Seckford in Westgate Street. At its base is the sundial from Smart's Wharf on the docks, inscribed 'Why stand you here idle while time passes'.

This was another prosperous period for the town, the port being used by many wealthy merchants. At the bottom of the hanging are depicted, from left to right, the merchant's mark of Thomas Pownder and the coats of arms of Henry Toolye, the Merchant Adventurers and William Smart, with the merchant's mark of Thomas Drayll on the far right.

The ship on the river, the *Mary Walsingham*, belonged to Henry Tooley, a merchant fishing in Icelandic waters. The smaller ship, the *Desire*, took Thomas Cavendish of Trimley and Thomas Eldred of Ipswich around the world in the 1560s. The grampusses, or porpoises, were washed up further down the Orwell. As they traditionally belonged to the king, their tails and fins were cut off and sent to him in London.

On the wharf to the right of Wolsey's Gate is the inner court of the Isaac Lord building, well restored today. Between this and the Quay is the magnificent hall and meeting place of the Merchant Adventurers which also remains. The other buildings are from Brown's Yard.

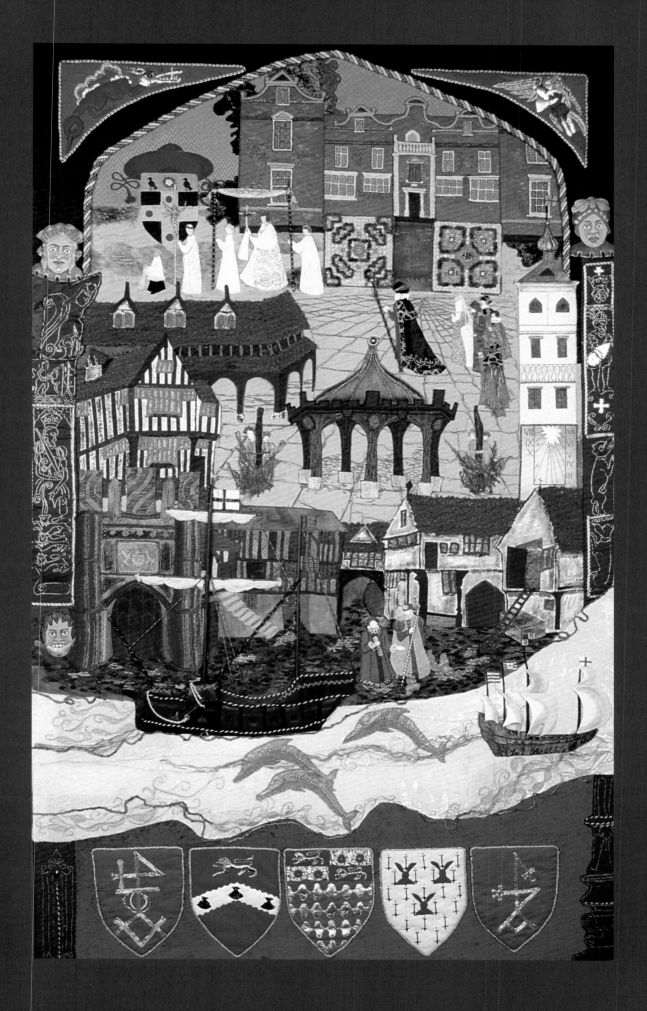

The Stuarts

During the early seventeenth century there was fresh religious strife in Ipswich. Easy access to the Low Countries had long enabled the writings of the reformers Luther, Calvin and Zwingli to be smuggled in to the town. The town preacher from 1605, Samuel Ward, an influential advocate of plain worship and bible-based sermons, was twice imprisoned for offending the king and his bishops. He was accused of encouraging townsfolk to emigrate to Puritan New England, and the *Godspeed* moored by the wharf took some of them as early as 1602. Below the corner post on the left-hand side from a house in Carr Street is the 'Watch Ward' Armada beacon from Samuel Ward's portrait in Ipswich Museum.

The town was firmly on the Roundhead side in the Civil Wars which led to the beheading of King Charles I. To the left of the Ipswich coat of arms at the top of the panel is an anti-papal drawing from the Museum and on the right the Prince of Wales feathers from St Margaret's Church – a secret sign of loyalty to Charles II during the Commonwealth. Cromwell's government disappointed many people and the town was entirely ready to welcome the restored monarch Charles II in 1660. Music, drama, dance and colour reappeared in everyday life, as shown at the foot of the panel. New Corporation regalia were made and the silver-gilt mace is shown on the right. The Ancient House in the Buttermarket, prominent in this scene and made by combining several much earlier dwellings, is an enduring celebration of the Restoration. The Sparrowes showed their loyalty by placing new Royal Arms on the house front as well as the depicting the four known continents in elaborate pargetting. Dial Lane at the side of the house was the junction of the butter market, to the right, and the fish market, to the left, which Sparrowe eventually had removed.

The larger figures on the left and right are a prominent merchant of the time, John Knapp, and his wife Martha.

On the left of the panel, above the Neptune, can be seen the medieval West Gate opposite the Shire Hall, built in 1699.

Notice that the river starts to become polluted on this panel and continues to be so until towards the end of the last panel.

The Georgians

The Georgian period in Ipswich was one of economic decline.

The arch at the top of the hanging is the carving from the Ipswich Coffee House, which stood at the bottom of Tower Street. It is now over the entrance to Cliff House (the Brewery Tap) at Cliff Quay.

On either side of the carving is shown mechanism from the clock of St Margaret's Church reminding us that clock-making was important in the town. On the left is a long-case clock by Moore of Ipswich, now in Christchurch Mansion.

The arch doubles as a proscenium arch and the green areas below become the flats with foliage from the theatre in Tacket Street where David Garrick made his debut in 1741.

Within the arch is the Georgian Provision Market (north of Falcon Street) with a drinking fountain in front of it on the left. Below, the stage coach shows that such travel began this century.

The fine Unitarian Meeting House (to the right) stands today beside the new Willis Corroon building. Its wonderful carved pulpit (below) is thought to have come from the workshop of Grinling Gibbons.

The Old Custom House (beside the grandfather clock) was Tudor and fronted, to the right, by a crane building. Further to the right is the naval dockyard, and behind there is gravestone with the Hebrew word Shalom (Peace) on it, representing the Jewish cemetery first used this century.

Neat fields on the southern side of the river are taken from a painting in the Town Hall. The large pigs would soon have found their way to market near the Provision Market!

On the left is Tom Peartree, copied from the painting which Gainsborough stood in his own garden as a joke. Thomas Gainsborough brought his new young wife to live in Ipswich in about 1750.

Close to the river is the racecourse which existed until 1902. The windmill to the right is Stoke Mill, long taken down. Behind it is a vat from Cobbold's Brewery.

The Victorian Period

The importance of Cornhill is again emphasised on this panel. Its clearance must have been very dramatic with the removal of the Market Cross and the Moot Hall in 1812. The Hall was replaced by a new Town Hall in 1818. A second, larger (and present) Town Hall replaced it in 1867, seen at the top, right.

To the left of the Town Hall is the old Three Tuns Tavern, soon to be demolished to make way for Princes Street. On the other side is the Golden Lion Hotel, still there today. Below this is the tower of the new building of Ipswich School in Henley Road which opened in 1852. Above, in the right- hand corner are the lovely Minton tiles with their Madonna lilies adorning the sedilia in St Mary le Tower Church. The spire and tower of the church hold centre ground in the hanging. It was the civic church and the people of Ipswich met in the churchyard to elect their town government after King John granted the Charter in 1200. It was almost totally rebuilt during the Victorian period.

Bethesda Church, erected by a Gloucester alderman in memory of his mother who was baptised in the River Orwell at the age of fifteen, is shown below Tower Church, although in reality it stands at the bottom of Fonnereau Road.

To the right is the Ragged School, built by the Quakers for the education of the poor, and later moved to its present building in Waterworks Street. The shops to the right are again in Fore Street, opposite the Neptune Inn. Above these buildings is one of the many horse buses which would have been parked on the Cornhill. Below the Fore Street shops are small lanes and cottages near to the Docks and towards Rope Walk which were slum-cleared in the 1950s. On the dockside is the new (1845) Custom House which still stands. At the far right-hand end is the Victorian warehouse with the maltings behind, taken from a contemporary picture of the docks. To the left is the railway with its tunnel (the first to be built with a curve in it) which opened in 1845. It demonstrates the importance of Ipswich's newly founded industries linking them to the docks and trade routes. The top left-hand corner of the panel has a bracket from Ipswich Station platform. Goods to and from the railway were transported by horse and cart, shown on the quayside. In front of the Customs House in the dock are two Ipswich barges, used to bring coal in (on the left) and take agricultural goods out.

Inside the left-hand arch is the 1810 Corn Exchange. In 1881 the site was re-used for the Post Office, now Lloyds TSB. In the area below can be seen representations of one of the important manufacturing firms in Victorian Ipswich, the first plough and lawnmower made by Ransomes. Below them to the left are the livery stables of Fred Smith, still standing in Princes Street.

At the bottom of the panel are the County Courts of 1837, currently County Hall. The Scotsman on the left stood outside Finlay's tobacconist at the junction of Crown Street and Westgate Street. Anyone who grew up in Ipswich after the Second World War would have known this statue which is an advertisement for Churchman's cigarettes, made in the town. It is now in Christchurch Mansion. On the opposite side is a Suffolk Yeoman. The military in the town garrison would have been important in the nineteenth century.

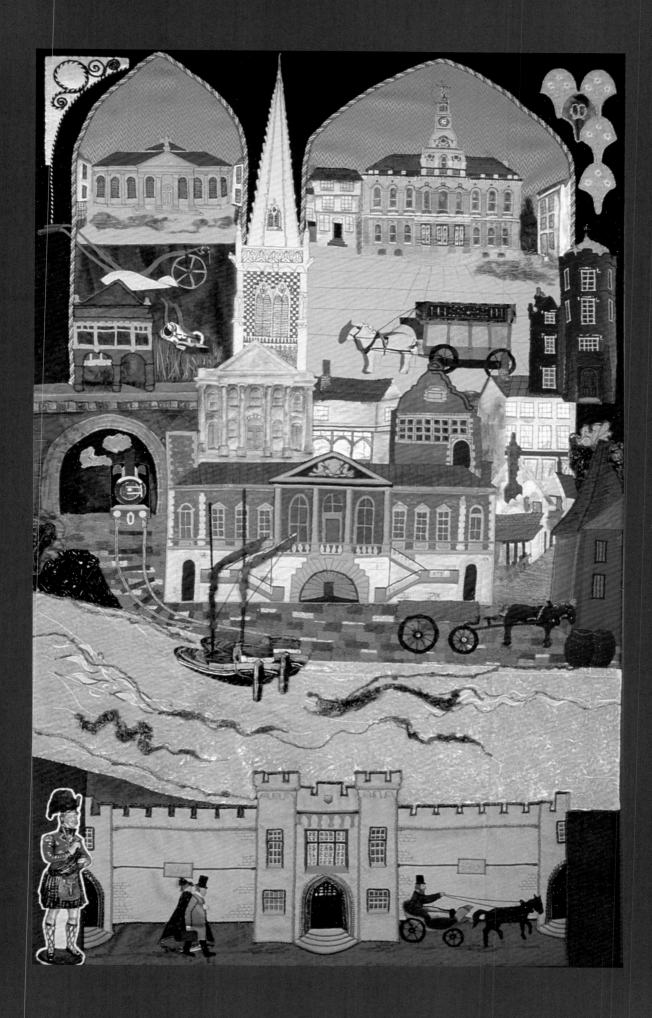

The Twentieth Century

The last hanging was almost the most difficult to design with so many changes to reflect in just one hundred years.

The hanging reads from left to right in time. At the top of the left-hand side is the window of the Central Library in Northgate Street, designed by Munro Cautley in 1924, and below this is the Pretty's lingerie factory, symbolic of the many clothing and other factories in the town early in the century. Below this is the Victorian warehouse on the dock front belonging to Paul's which is still operational. The old docks have had wide-ranging changes: from being a bustling, active manual area to a mechanised complex they are now becoming a leisure centre. The building next to Paul's is the former Contship building and to the right an old Victorian warehouse. The original Cobbold's Maltings next to this is now a pub. The old dock is now mainly devoted to pleasure craft, hence the sailing boat and cruiser on the river.

Above Paul's building on the left is the 1920s tower of St Thomas's Church in Bramford Lane and next to it on the right the late Victorian tower of All Saints Church, both built in the outer rim of the spreading town.

The Art Deco period is represented by Broomhill Swimming Baths and the building at the bottom of St Margaret's Plain, now Kwik Fit (to the right of the churches in the hanging). Below to the right is the entrance to the Buttermarket complex near the site of the old Provision Market. On the extreme right is Suffolk College, originally the Civic College, built in the 1960s.

To the left at the top is the arch entrance to Lloyds Avenue, linking Tower Ramparts to Cornhill. In the centre is the 'Ship' sculpture by Bernard Reynolds, distinguished artist and lecturer at Ipswich School of Art, now in Civic Drive close to The Wolsey Theatre, featured on the right.

At the top to the left is the award –winning black glass building designed by Norman Foster for Willis Faber and Dumas, now Willis Corroon, built after Civic Drive was cleared in the 1960s. Below is the Ipswich Town Football Club built on the old town marshes, formerly a grazing area belonging to the Ipswich Portmen. The Cenotaph, a memorial to those who fell in the First World War, stands in Christchurch Park.

The top left corner has the symbol of the Congregation of Jesus and Mary which came to Ipswich 150 years ago to assist in the education of orphans. The top right corner has a decoration from the Corporation Plate designed by Gerald Benney in 1963 and presented by Mr Goodwin whose family ran Stoke Windmill (see the Georgian panel). The cross represents Stoke Windmill and the three prongs symbolise the three main industries connected with Ipswich: the port, agriculture, and engineering.

The River Orwell flows to the sea under the new Orwell Bridge, built in 1982, with HMS Grafton, adopted by Ipswich, sailing along it. Notice the water gets cleaner towards the right, reflecting efforts made to clear the river of pollution.

The Spitfire flying above the river was one of many based in the area during the Second World War. On the left of the river is the old Power Station, now demolished, and beside it a drag crane, another example of the important heavy industry in the town. The large container ship symbolises the new era of trade in the West Bank terminal area with the port cranes to the right.

Acknowledgements

I should like to thank all the team for their hard work and support in the creation of the Charter Hangings.

The following worked on the hangings:

L BENCE	J GOODMAN	C NORMAN
U BAILLIE	B GRIMALDI	B PACKER
P CATTON	J HAYLOCK	M RASMUSSEN
A CLOKE	E HODGSON	P ROWELL
V CONNELL	C HUTT	C SUTHERLAND
S CRANWELL	M INGHAM	N TALLIN
M CUDDIFORD	L KINCAID	S TAYLOR
N DEMETRIADI	S LUCKING	J THOMAS
R DICKINSON	V MACGREGOR	B WALSH
L EMLY	J MERCER	
S GIDDINGS	M NIGHTINGALE	

Assisted by:

C ARNOLD	M CHILVERS	K GLUSHKO
J BRUCE	S DUFF	S READ
J BLURTON	R FLECK	M TEMME

All the different panels were assembled in Suffolk College and I am so grateful that we were able to use the workshops at odd times and in the holidays.

I should like to thank Ipswich Arts Association for their support in the project, especially Professor Chris Green, Barry Salmon, Ivan Gilson, and Frances Gilson; Dr John Blatchly for his advice and support; John Freer for making the frames for the hangings; Anne Parry for her patience and forbearance in editing this book and, finally, I thank my husband for putting up with me and the chaos I create!

Isabel Clover pictured with the Pre-Charter and Charter hangings.
Photograph reproduced by kind permission of the East Anglian Daily Times.